EPIC BOOKS are no ordinary books. They burst with intense action, high-speed heroics, and shadows of the unknown. Are you ready for an Epic adventure?

This edition first published in 2024 by Bellwether Media, Inc.

No part of this publication may be reproduced in whole or in part without written permission of the publisher. For information regarding permission, write to Bellwether Media, Inc., Attention: Permissions Department, 6012 Blue Circle Drive, Minnetonka, MN 55343.

Library of Congress Cataloging-in-Publication Data

Names: Duling, Kaitlyn, author.
Title: Ferrari 296 GTB / by Kaitlyn Duling.
Description: Minneapolis, MN : Bellwether Media, 2024. | Series: Cool cars | Includes bibliographical references and index. | Audience: Ages 7-12 | Audience: Grades 2-3 | Summary: "Engaging images accompany information about the Ferrari 296 GTB. The combination of high-interest subject matter and light text is intended for students in grades 2 through 7"--Provided by publisher.
Identifiers: LCCN 2023001643 (print) | LCCN 2023001644 (ebook) | ISBN 9798886874983 | ISBN 9798886876864 (ebook)
Subjects: LCSH: Ferrari 296 GTB--Juvenile literature. | Sports cars--Juvenile literature.
Classification: LCC TL215.F47 D85 2024 (print) | LCC TL215.F47 (ebook) | DDC 629.222/2--dc23/eng/20230113
LC record available at https://lccn.loc.gov/2023001643
LC ebook record available at https://lccn.loc.gov/2023001644

Text copyright © 2024 by Bellwether Media, Inc. EPIC and associated logos are trademarks and/or registered trademarks of Bellwether Media, Inc.

Editor: Rachael Barnes   Designer: Jeffrey Kollock

Printed in the United States of America, North Mankato, MN.

TABLE OF CONTENTS

A POWERFUL PLUG-IN	4
ALL ABOUT THE 296 GTB	6
PARTS OF THE 296 GTB	12
THE 296 GTB'S FUTURE	20
GLOSSARY	22
TO LEARN MORE	23
INDEX	24

A POWERFUL PLUG-IN »

A driver heads home in their Ferrari 296 GTB. They zip around tight turns. At home, they plug in the car to charge.

ALL ABOUT THE 296 GTB »

FERRARI RACE CAR

ENZO FERRARI

Enzo Ferrari was a race car driver. He founded the Ferrari company in Italy. He started building race cars in the 1940s.

The F40 and 458 became well-known **models**.

LONG-TIME WINNERS
Ferrari is the most successful Formula One racing team in history. They have been racing since 1950!

FERRARI 458

📍 WHERE IS IT MADE?

EUROPE

MARANELLO, ITALY

It is a **supercar** that was built for the road. The 296 GTB can drive up to 205 miles (330 kilometers) per hour!

296 GTB BASICS

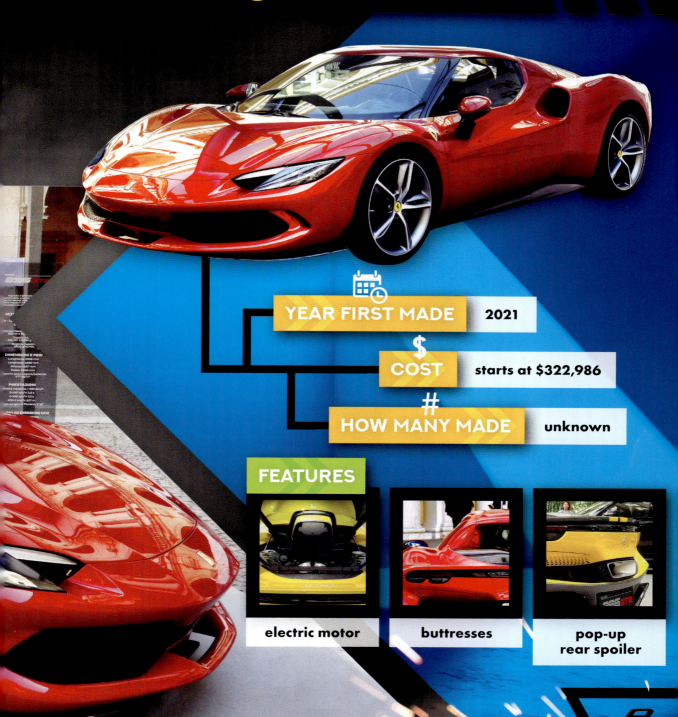

YEAR FIRST MADE 2021

COST starts at $322,986

HOW MANY MADE unknown

FEATURES

electric motor | buttresses | pop-up rear spoiler

The 296 GTB has parts similar to older Ferrari models.

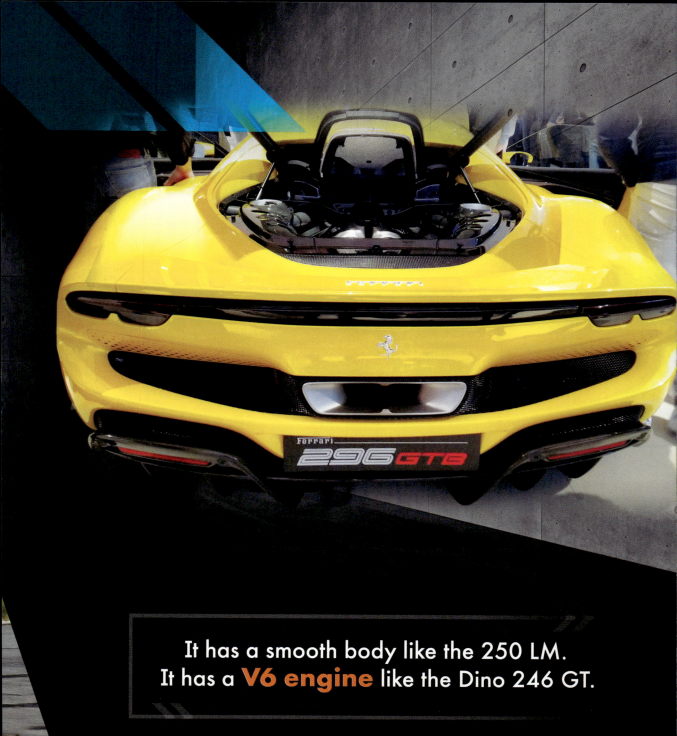

It has a smooth body like the 250 LM. It has a **V6 engine** like the Dino 246 GT.

PARTS OF THE 296 GTB »

The 296 GTB has a V6 engine and an **electric motor**. Together, they produce 819 **horsepower**!

Drivers can press a button to turn off the engine. This lets them use the electric motor on its own.

ENGINE SPECS

HYBRID TWIN-TURBO V6 ENGINE AND ELECTRIC MOTOR »

TOP SPEED — 205 miles (330 kilometers) per hour

0-62 TIME — 2.9 seconds

HORSEPOWER — 819 hp

The 296 GTB is **aerodynamic**. Air flows past the **buttresses**. A rear **spoiler** can pop up. It helps the car grip the road.

BUTTRESS ›››

SIZE CHART

WIDTH 77.1 inches (195.8 centimeters)

Owners can choose a **convertible** model. The 296 GTS has a folding roof!

296 GTS

HEIGHT 46.7 inches (118.7 centimeters)

LENGTH 179.7 inches (456.5 centimeters)

RACING RED

Early racing rules said Italian cars had to be painted red. It was a winning color! Ferrari still paints many of its cars Rosso Corsa, or racing red.

Owners can **customize** their 296 GTB. They can choose paint colors and wheels.

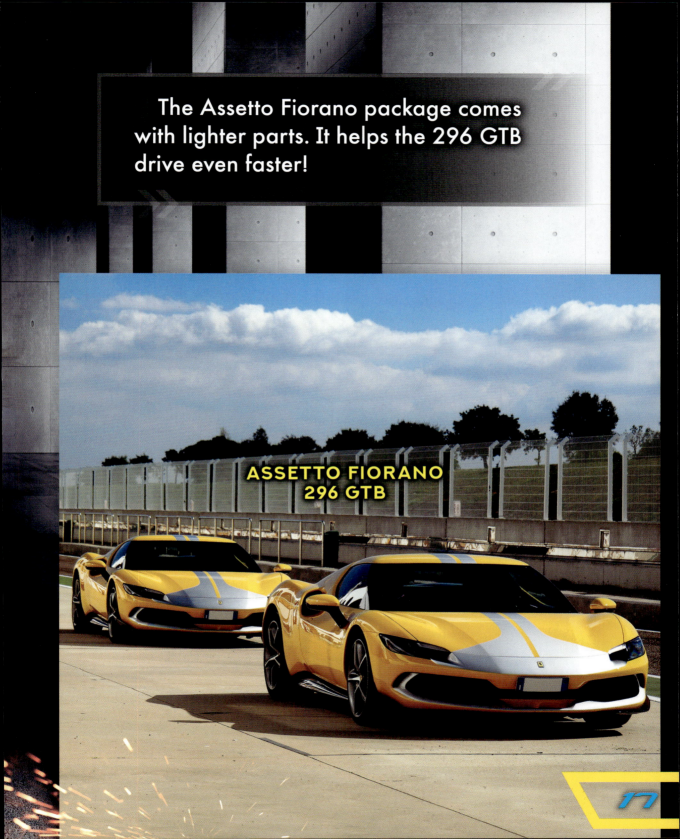

The Assetto Fiorano package comes with lighter parts. It helps the 296 GTB drive even faster!

A button on the steering wheel starts the 296 GTB.

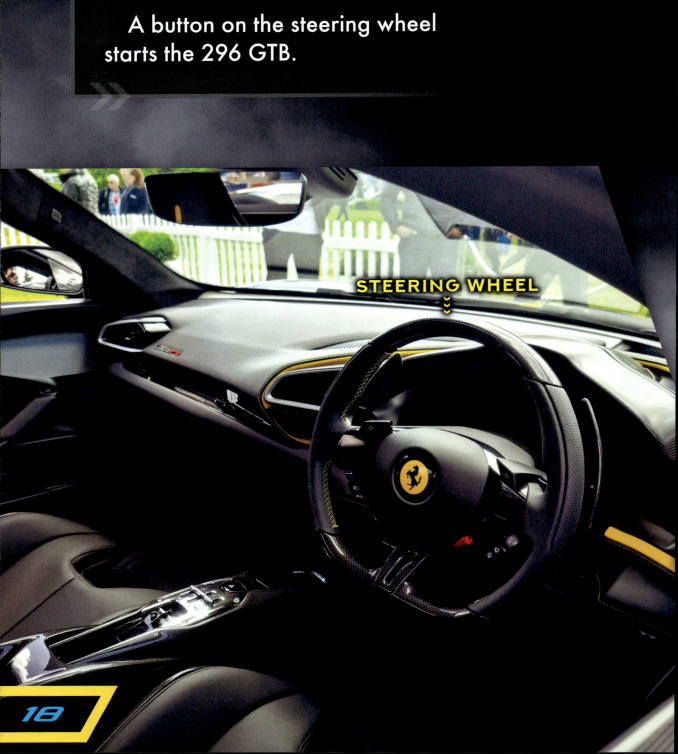

STEERING WHEEL

PASSENGER CONTROL SCREEN

A special screen behind the steering wheel shows information for the driver. It shows speed and driving directions. The passenger has a control screen, too.

THE 296 GTB'S FUTURE »

The 296 GTB will not be the last hybrid Ferrari! The company plans to make more hybrid and electric cars.

An all-electric car is planned for 2025. Ferrari hopes these powerful plug-in cars will be a hit!

MORE DOORS

Ferrari announced its first four-door car in 2022. It will be bigger than Ferraris of the past.

GLOSSARY

aerodynamic—able to move through air easily

buttresses—parts on a car that add support and direct air around it

convertible—a car with a folding or soft roof

customize—to make to personal order

electric motor—a machine that gives something the power to move by using electricity

horsepower—a measurement of the power of an engine or motor

hybrid—a car that uses both a gasoline engine and an electric motor for power

models—specific kinds of cars

spoiler—a part on the back of a car that helps the car grip the road

supercar—an expensive and high-performing sports car

V6 engine—an engine with 6 cylinders arranged in the shape of a "V"

TO LEARN MORE

AT THE LIBRARY

Hamilton, S.L. *The World's Fastest Cars.* Minneapolis, Minn.: Abdo Publishing, 2021.

Sommer, Nathan. *Ferrari 812 Superfast.* Minneapolis, Minn.: Bellwether Media, 2023.

Swanson, Jennifer. *How Do Hybrid Cars Work?* Mankato, Minn.: The Child's World, 2022.

ON THE WEB

FACTSURFER

Factsurfer.com gives you a safe, fun way to find more information.

1. Go to www.factsurfer.com.

2. Enter "Ferrari 296 GTB" into the search box and click 🔍.

3. Select your book cover to see a list of related content.

INDEX

aerodynamic, 14
Assetto Fiorano, 17
basics, 9
body, 11
buttresses, 14
colors, 16
control screen, 19
convertible, 15
electric cars, 20
electric motor, 12
engine, 11, 12
engine specs, 12
Ferrari (company), 6, 7, 16, 20, 21
Ferrari, Enzo, 6
future, 20, 21
history, 6, 7, 8
horsepower, 12
hybrid, 5, 20

Italy, 6, 7
models, 7, 10, 11, 15
racing, 6, 7, 16
road, 7, 8, 14
roof, 15
size chart, 14–15
speed, 5, 8, 17, 19
spoiler, 14
steering wheel, 18, 19
supercar, 8
wheels, 16

The images in this book are reproduced through the courtesy of: Alexandre Prevot, front cover; Calreyn88, p. 3; Roman Belogorodov, p. 4; Jason Harris/ Alamy, pp. 5, 17; Ev. Safronov, p. 6; Public Domain, p. 6 (Enzo Ferrari); Brandon Woyshnis, p. 7; Fabrizio Annovi, pp. 8-9, 9 (buttresses), 14, 16; fabrizio annovi/ Alamy, p. 9; Y.Leclercq, pp. 9 (electric motor), 11 (electric motor), 12 (engine), 19; pelican-actor, pp. 9 (spoiler), 15; CJM Photography/ Alamy, p. 10; Martyn Lucy/ Contributor/ Getty Images, pp. 13, 14 (width), 20, 21; Semir Sakic, p. 15 (length); Jaimie Wilson, p. 18.